ALL I WANT FOR CHRISTMAS

Edited by

Becki Mee

First published in Great Britain in 1999 by
POETRY NOW
1-2 Wainman Road, Woodston,
Peterborough, PE2 7BU
Telephone (01733) 230746
Fax (01733) 230751

All Rights Reserved

Copyright Contributors 1999

HB ISBN 0 75430 602 X
SB ISBN 0 75430 603 8

FOREWORD

Although we are a nation of poetry writers we are accused of not reading poetry and not buying poetry books: after many years of listening to the incessant gripes of poetry publishers, I can only assume that the books they publish, in general, are books that most people do not want to read.

Poetry should not be obscure, introverted, and as cryptic as a crossword puzzle: it is the poet's duty to reach out and embrace the world.

The world owes the poet nothing and we should not be expected to dig and delve into a rambling discourse searching for some inner meaning.

The reason we write poetry (and almost all of us do) is because we want to communicate: an ideal; an idea; or a specific feeling. Poetry is as essential in communication, as a letter; a radio; a telephone, and the main criteria for selecting the poems in this anthology is very simple: they communicate.

CONTENTS

Zog The Frog	P E Jones	1
The Festive Season	Susan Mullinger	2
Jingle Bell Santa	Lauren Bell	3
A Diet For Santa	Tracy Bell	4
Christmas Spirit	Peter Davies	5
Sana Came In A UFO	Ann G Wallace	6
The Colourful Days	Ruth Daviat	8
Santa	J M Stoles	9
With A Heigh-Ho	Agnes McRae	10
Christmas	Martin Uprichard	11
Christmas Cheer	Pat Weeks Goodridge	12
Untitled	Maria Waters	13
A Second Hymn For The Little Ones	Sylvia Gorwill	14
The Catmas Tails	Donald Jay	15
Bengie Tabby Cat's First Christmas	Linda Brown	16
The Donkey	J M Service	17
Christmas	Mary Haslam	18
On Top	A G Simonds	19
Snowman	Derek J Morgan	20
Children's Christmas Verse	Jean P McGovern	21
Christmas Magic	Katrina Shepherd	22
Little Donkey	Dennis Packham	23
Children's Christmas Verse	Ghazanfer Eqbal	24
Hope	Phillip A Taylor	25
The School Christmas Party	Lorna June Burdon	26
How Much I Love Christmas	Rebecca Haslam	27
Poor Daddy Christmas	Gabby Copperstone	28
A Pun For Christmas	Roger Williams	29
Christmas	Eileen Kyte	30
Santa's Poem	Joanna Till	31
Dickie's Brick	Gary J Cox	32
Christmas Bazaar	Jennifer Bailey	33
One Night I Lay Wondering . . .	Margaret Gregory	34

The Bearded Fatman	Keith Farley	35
The Magic Of Christmas	Maureen Atkin	36
Christmas Lights	Ivy Allpress	38
Hickory Dickory Socks	Marisha Rose	39
Christmas Is Near	Jacqueline Darts	40
Christmas Time	Julie Birkenfield	41
A Christmas Poem	Kelly Duncan	42
Christmas	Louise Lothian	43
Santa	Sean Smith	44
Christmas List	Julie Cranston	45
Christmas	Natalie Lennox	46
What If?	Christopher Leith	47
Good Cheer	Thomas W Splitt	48
It's Christmas Again	Shaune Carey	49
Christmas	Vicky Harbour	50
Christmas	Lewanne Mudd	51
Christmas	Jonathan Wilcox	52
A Christmas Poem	Robert Prior	53
Christmas In Bloom	David E W Walker	54
Happy Christmas	Catriona McNicoll	55
I Don't Like Sprouts	Jessica Sutton	56
It's Christmas Time	Kirsty Williams	57
Christmas Is Near!	Jazzy H	58
The Christmas Brainstorm	Sarah Fox	59
It's Christmas Time	Ashley Jeggo	60
A Christmas Poem	Sarah Bolton	61
Christmas Poem	Rachel Halcrow	62
Christmas Poem	Sian Major	63
On Christmas Eve Long Ago	Douglas Beattie	64
Christmastime	Matthew Willis	65
The Band Comes	Richard Stoker	66
Happy Christmas Mother	Janet Hewitt	67
From Charlette's Ark To Jesus Christ	Charlette de Christi	68
Children's Christmas Verse	G A Pocock	69
Christmas Is Here	Laura Jane Cumming	70
Santa	Colin Kwok	71
It Is Christmas	Deen Lawrence	72

Christmas	Kevin Filmer	73
Santa's Grotto	Annette Carver	74
Singing Yo-Ho-Ho From Santa!	Hilary Jill Robson	75
Christmas Eve	N Carruthers	76
My Maker Is Greater Than My Daddy/Mommy!	Ciel	77
Popo The Clown Meets Santa	Sheila Valerie Baldwin	78
Christmastime	Betty Green	80
Our Christmas Eve	B R Lloyd	81
Santa's Arrival	Kay Rainsley	82
Auntie Blodwen's Christmas	Elizabeth Meredith	83
Christmas Magic	M Lister	84
Christmas Is For Life!	Denis Martindale	85
The Night Before Christmas	Julia Whale	86
Red And White	P J Littlefield	88
Anything Else You'd Like To Know About Xmas?	I M Brown	89
Christmas Eve	Marian Curtis Jones	90
Stay Cool Santa!	C Sanderson	91
Christmas Eve	Denise Russell	92
Untitled	Matthew James	93
Christmas Surprise	Pam Cook	94
Christmas Tree Song	Linda Anne Landers	95
If It Were Me	Patricia Cure	96
The Magi	Rosemary Keith	97
Thoughts About Christmas	Steven Donoghue	98

ZOG THE FROG

There once was a frog called Zog,
Who lived in a pond under a log.
Said Zog, one fine sunny day,
'I want to travel far far away.'
So he packed his bag,
Full of pond slime and swag,
And he started on his way.
He first came to a busy road,
Which was so wide and so broad.
As he hopped over
By a truck he was run over
Zog is alive no more
But in heaven he doth soar.
Poor poor little Zog,
The travelling frog.

P E Jones

THE FESTIVE SEASON

Season of tinsel and holly,
It is the time to be jolly.
Season to remember Christ's birth,
And celebrate his life on earth.
Season for decorative lights,
Time for children to stay up nights.
Season for many tiny treats,
With lots of chocolate to eat.

Susan Mullinger

JINGLE BELL SANTA

Jingle bells, Santa smells
Rudolph flew away,
Mrs Claus lost her draws
And they came back Christmas Day.

Lauren Bell (8)

A Diet For Santa

Santa Claus loves his grub,
His belly's as round as a Christmas pud,
Mrs Claus one day caused a riot,
By putting dear old Santa on a diet.

No more cookies, chocolates or mince pies,
'All those luxuries' she said *'You can kiss goodbye!'*
Santa Claus was very glum,
About the prospect of losing his jolly tum,

For breakfast instead of eggs and ham . . .
Now in front of him stood a bowl of dried up All Bran!
For dinner on his plate there now sat a lurking . . .
A mouldy shrivelled lettuce leaf and a pickled gherkin.

But the elves and the reindeer noticed . . .
That Santa had lost his sparkle,
Gone were his rosy cheeks
And his jolly chortle.

They went to Mrs Claus,
And loudly did complain,
That their dear old Santa Claus,
Was really not the same!

Mrs Claus then did relent,
Santa's special diet . . . out the window went,
To Santa's delight the very next day,
Ham and eggs for breakfast . . . on the table lay.

But Santa's learnt his lesson . . . about his jolly tum,
Now instead of eating two cookies . . . he only now eats one,
The rest he puts in a special box . . . he thinks it only fair,
That all the special treats he has . . . with the others he should share!

Tracy Bell

CHRISTMAS SPIRIT

As I'd been such a good little lad,
Father Christmas was ever so glad,
He tickled my tum,
And he cuddled my mum,
Then fell over - and swore like my dad!

Peter Davies

SANTA CAME IN A UFO

I looked through the window on Christmas Eve,
And much to my surprise,
Over the rooftops way up above,
There before my eyes,
By the light of the silvery moon,
No Santa's sleigh was in sight,
From my room all that I could see,
Hovering in the starry night,
Was a flying saucer with windows,
It was there I saw Santa inside,
Then suddenly he was gone,
Taking it for a ride,

Whoosh through the door into the hall,
At speed as the lights went flash,
Into bed I jumped as fast as I could,
It was then that I heard a loud crash,
Santa sat upon the floor,
His face like his coat quite red,
I looked at him, he looked at me,
Nothing between us was said,
In his hand he held instructions,
For driving the UFO,
Presents lay upon the floor,
As he nursed his bruised big toe,

Santa tried to stand to his feet,
Although a little unsteady,
Scattered all around him were,
Toy soldiers, dolls and a teddy,
He spied me there beneath the sheets,
He said that his Christmas sleigh,
Was in the garage way back home,
Having broken down that day,
When on his way from Jupiter,
On the way to the planet Mars,
He had been lent a UFO,
To travel back from the stars,

As Christmas time was not just,
For earth children he told me,
As all out in the vast universe,
Each have a Christmas tree,
The flying disc was a problem,
With a mind of its own Santa said,
Getting used to the controls,
And steering it straight ahead,
Especially when little Johnnie,
Who lives at number 54,
Leaves him a glass of sherry,
Near to his bedroom door,

Later that night all over England,
In a silver saucer I flew,
With Santa there at my side,
Not even my parents knew,
So if you saw helper,
That you thought was an elf,
Dressed in blue striped pyjamas,
I am afraid it was only myself.

Ann G Wallace

THE COLOURFUL DAYS

At Christmas time, with ice and snow
And glittering, towering tree
There's magic and I'm sure I know
There'll be December treats for me.
There seems to be a certain star
Rejoicing in the evening sky
And grown-ups somehow different are
As slowly winter hours pass by.
At school I love to splash the paint
With colours of the rainbow all
And teacher, patient as a saint,
Stands like a column, six feet tall.
No colour is like Christmas though,
Red especially warm and bright,
Silver and green the mistletoe
Quite fairy-like by candlelight.
The pretty pink and mauve balloons
Enchant the living room we know,
Decorative flowers, cardboard moons
Weird shadows on the curtains throw.
Gold round the mirror richly gleams,
Fiery garlands to celebrate
These happy moments though it seems
So difficult to have to wait.
Alluring shades excite me so -
Maybe we borrow heaven's bliss,
Its sovereignty and gorgeous glow,
God's wonder at a time like this.

Ruth Daviat

SANTA

Hark the herald angels sing
Come and eat a chicken wing
Peace on earth and mercy mild
Santa delivers gifts to every child
Joyful all ye nations rise
See the reindeers
Fly across the sky
With the angels' host proclaim
Christ was born in Bethlehem
Hark the herald angels sing
Santa's eating a chicken wing.

J M Stoles

WITH A HEIGH-HO

Santa lay stretched out beside the firelight glow
His large tummy rising and falling with each deep snore,
Long flowing beard and whiskers were as white as snow
And his ruddy face the colour of red apples shone.

Outside the window his reindeer were in dismay
Pushing, stamping, peering in at Santa,
Till he wakened with a start in total disarray
With many things to do before the night's well started.

He pulled his shiny boots on with much haste and speed
And coat and hat he did adorn were really made for him,
To tweak and twirl his moustache he felt there was a need
Before swinging his sack with presents full upon his back.

The snow was falling thick and fast on this Christmas Eve
He quickly pulled on the reins causing bells a jingling,
They galloped away into the night their mysterious paths to weave
In the dead of night with only stars to guide him.

Skimming through the glistening snow, Santa was elated
The cackling geese and snowy owls were there to see them
                                              on their way,
With a heigh-ho! They were thrust into the air now ascended
Leaving hills and woodlands, houses, church and steeple.

The moon escaped the darkened clouds as fast the sleigh did move,
Above the silhouette was clear against the brilliant orb,
'Little children do not fear, I love to rant and rave
And fill the stockings full with many brightly coloured toys.'

Agnes McRae

CHRISTMAS

Christmas is a time to be jolly,
My mum gets pricked by holly,
Santa's got a little helper,
My dog can make him scamper,
Now this story starts to descend,
When Santa rubs his back end.

Martin Uprichard (11)

Christmas Cheer

Bradley's got his Action Man,
And Daniel's got a 'Pute,' (computer)
Lloyd has got his BMX
It cost a lot of loot!
Charlotte's got her Barbie doll,
And Alia, a Ted,
Thomas' chuffed with everything,
And Grace has gone to bed!
Liam's very happy,
Mum and Dad relieved,
Granny's put her teeth back in,
And Grandad's fast asleep!
The cat has noshed on turkey,
The dog's been for a run,
Everyone is stuffed with food,
Let's stick the telly on!
Oh, wot a lovely Christmas!
O, wot a hoot it's been!
Uncle Fred got drunk again,
And Aunty watched the Queen,
Still everybody's happy,
So what more can we say,
We'll do it all again next year,
Hip-hip, hip-hip, hooray!

Pat Weeks Goodridge

UNTITLED

You spent all day making a snowman tall
Waited all year for the snow to fall
You've dressed him up, made him fine
But then Mum calls, it's that time
Then off to bed you must go
But have you ever wondered,
What goes on in the snow?
Cuddled up quite warm,
Tucked in tight, late at night.
Outside, the snowmen begin to swarm
In your back yard, maybe tonight
And if you went out you'd have a fright
For jellies and ice-cream are all around
And snowmen come from off their ground
To dance and play and have some fun
Enjoying themselves until the morning sun
But if you get up in the middle of the night
And turn on the light
If you look outside, what will you see?
Not a dozen snowmen, not even three
The moment that you raise your head
The moment you step out of bed
The snowmen know that you are there
And back to their gardens they go with care
To wait for you for the very next day
Ready for you, to come out and play

Maria Waters

A Second Hymn For The Little Ones

Such a bright bright star, shining way up in the sky,
And we wonder what it means when we look up high, up high.
It reminds us of the star which shone many years ago
To tell us of a baby's birth, our Jesus Christ, you know.

Such a clear, clear moon, shining with a radiant light
And we wonder what it means when it shines so bright, so bright.
It reminds us of the one which shone over Bethlehem
Where Jesus' mother was so quietly nursing him.

Such a 'Ding, dong, ding' as the church bells ring and ring,
And we wonder what it means when people sing and sing.
It reminds us of the bells which did sound o'er all the earth
To tell the wondrous story of our Baby Jesus' birth.

Jesus was born on Christmas Day,
Jesus or friend and Saviour.

Sylvia Gorwill

THE CATMAS TAILS

Oh little town of Catton how sweet we see you sleep,
As through the dark streets and onto the roofs Santa Paws creeps,
He carries a large sack he climbs down all your chimneys
To bring Catmas gifts to all your cats.
Rabbit and fish treats and Victorian chocolate mice
As around the Catmas Tree the cats sing Catols all night.
In the bleak mid winter the frosty winds do blow,
As around the fire our cats are nice and warm,
And now our cats smell turkey cooking on the stove.
They know they will get some if like you children they are very good.
Oh little town of Catton I can see you no more
You have completely vanished beneath all that snow oh oh oh.
Our cats will not go out they want to keep their tails all nice and
dry and warm,
In the bleak mid winter and not so long ago.
Catmas chants fill the air Cat-no-tus Nar-tus floats around everywhere,
To celebrate the birth of Christ the King
In church, chapel and monastery, the sounds of praise to Christ the
King.
Midnight Mass, hymns and cat chants ring out all across the land
Like waves of sound against the sand.
Enchanted catols, music in the streets, church bells, hand bells
ring ring ring to celebrate the birth of Christ the King,
Sing lustily and with good courage sing,
Tell the world the good news that Jesus Christ came to this world
for us to save.
Traditional music fills the air Cat-no-tus Nar-tus
Everywhere music boxes ring out with tunes to tell the world
of the birth of Christ the King.
He came for the poor sinner to save
Believe in Jesus and be saved.
God the Father, Son and Holy Ghost bless this time of remembrance,
Catmas time should be a time of joy to cats and people everywhere.

Donald Jay

BENGIE TABBY CAT'S FIRST CHRISTMAS

Well into the midst of winter, deep snow under paw
Bengie Tabby Cat was excited, he'd never seen Christmas before
Christmas decorations had been delivered, to his home the store
Along with children's toys, games and gift wrappings galore

Joined by cousin Rupert Black Cat, they decided to climb a tree
Caught by the owner, both put outside and told to leave things be
Little faces pressed close to the window, how they wanted to play
They hatched a plot to meet in the store, at close of day

After his fish supper, his mother Tabatha put him to bed
Kissing him she said go to sleep, but he had other ideas instead
He waited until it was quiet, then crept down to the store
Reaching up for the lock, he let Rupert in the front door

Their tails flapped with excitement, eyes filled with glee
They decided to race each other, to the top of a Christmas tree
Rupert unrolled ribbons, Bengie kicked baubles on the floor
Bengie miaowed, oh what fun, we couldn't wish for anything more

Until noticing a red leather collar, with a little gold bell
Oh how he wanted to have it, on him it would look swell
He jumped up to reach it, knocking the display to the ground
Waking both his parents up, with the terrible sound

Seeing what had happened, Toby and Tabatha both saw red
Sending cousin Rupert home, Bengie was scolded and put to bed
Bengie knew he'd been naughty, there would be a punishment
He would have no Christmas present, even if one was sent

Bengie had promised to be good, it was now Christmas Eve
Hanging his stocking when going to bed, not expecting to receive
Awakened from his catnap, he couldn't believe his eyes
The red leather collar was in his stocking, what a nice surprise

It would be a happy Christmas, taking the collar in his paws
Reading the label he knew, he'd been forgiven by Santa Claus

Linda Brown

THE DONKEY
(Dedicated to the children of St Mark's School, Godalming, Surrey)

The donkey carried Mary the maid
over the desert sand,
And in the place where he set his hooves
sprang flowers in the Holy Land.

The shepherds followed the flowery path
to the place where the young child lay.
They found a grey donkey, and Mary the maid,
and a baby who slept in the hay.

If you close your eyes, you will see the child,
and his mother, Mary the maid.
You will see the flowers that will bloom for all time
in the straw where the donkey laid.

J M Service

CHRISTMAS

Santa's coming soon hooray!
I hope I get lots of toys,
He only likes to give them out,
To good little girls and boys.

So I'm being a little angel,
Till the big day comes around,
I'll try my best to please him,
My head's in the air
My feet on the ground.

I might not get all the things that I want,
But will be thankful for what he leaves,
Only he can decide if I'm asking too much,
As the bag on his back he heaves.

I know he'll leave me one or two,
If I'm good then maybe three,
Or even leave me four or five,
Wouldn't that be lucky me!

Mary Haslam

ON TOP

You look at me and say aah
        My silken dress is by far
The best you've ever seen
        But that hasn't always been.

Born a humble doll in fifty nine
        Just six inches tall, features fine,
A little blonde girl called Sally
        Gave me the pretty name of Carlie.

For two years I was her only joy
        I was number one over every toy
But then a Barbie came one day
        And little Carlie was thrown away.

Her mum feeling sorry for me
        Said 'You'd be perfect for the tree,'
With a piece of white silk bright,
        My gorgeous dress was made that night.

Tinsel my fair hair did adorn
        A loving fairy was born,
Pipe cleaner with silver star, my wand
        So finally, I was transformed.

Now each Christmas for thirty years
        I have watched through laughter and tears
Sally grow from child to lady
        And have her own girl baby.

And as they all smile at me
        I'll smile back, for you see
Love is the only thing
        Needed for Christmas to bring.

A G Simmonds

SNOWMAN

I saw a great big snowman
        Upon the village green
It was the biggest snowman
        That I had ever seen.

With a red silk hat upon his head
        Two eyes made out of coal
A cheeky smile upon his face
        He looked a happy soul.

A broom tucked in beneath his arm
        And a carrot for his nose
A pipe stuck in-between his teeth
        And the smoke about him rose.

An old blue scarf around his neck,
        Kept out the winter chill,
And every time I touched him
        It gave me quite a thrill.

I danced around that snowman
        Until the break of day,
Then the sun it smiled upon him
        And he slowly went away.

Derek J Morgan

CHILDREN'S CHRISTMAS VERSE

Santa will travel afar on Christmas Eve Day
Jingling the bells in his merry old way
But, he gets into a few scrapes 'Oh oh'
But, soon will be skipping the traffic jams 'Oh ho'

He drives yet again, on the snowy road
The reindeers' ears prick up, as they carry the load
Of wrapped up presents, and lots of toys
For good little girls, and good little boys

Things just happen, while the snow is falling
His sleigh breaks down, because Santa is speeding
The servicemen came to fix the sleigh just in time
So, Santa drives carefully, jingling the bells in rhyme

At last he arrives and climbs down the chimney breast
Now, could this be some joke, or just a zest
As Santa gets stuck, but comes down very slow
While, the reindeers are staring through the window

Now, his beard has gone black, instead of white
It really looks a sight, but Santa is alright
Please children, do not go outside to have a peep
Because all good children should be fast asleep

As Santa is in a hurry, for his reindeers are waiting
To be driven back again where the hard snow is falling
If you stay good over the festive seasons, and another year
'Ha ha', Santa will be back for more adventures, with good cheer.

Jean P McGovern

CHRISTMAS MAGIC

Jingling sleigh-bells like giggling elves
sing out through a bright, glittering sky
as Santa Claus and his reindeer friends
go merrily riding by.

Father Christmas is here to bring all children cheer
dressed in jolly red warm cosy cloak
he chortles with laughter as trusty reindeer
together share many good jokes.

Over sparkling roofs their galloping hooves
are led onwards by moonbeams and starlight
to take wondrous gifts to boys and girls
this magical winter's night.

Santa's smile glows from his head to his toes
his eyes are a twinkle with fun
he delves into his sack, with a chuckle of joy
finds a present for everyone.

His work is quite done as golden dawn sun
heralds time now for children to play
Christmas angels awake to give their special thanks
for a child born on this Christmas Day.

Katrina Shepherd

LITTLE DONKEY

Once I had a little donkey
Who loved to run and play
And I let him take me for a ride
One snowy Christmas Day
And as it was Christmas
I let him make his own way

He took me to a stable
There were hens and goats and sheep
And a baby in a manger
But he was not asleep
For as I bent over him
He whispered in my ear
And the words that he told me
Were oh so very clear

Now don't do wrong, always do right
Keep the peace and don't fight wars
Listen to my words my friend
And salvation shall be yours
I'll not forget that Christmas Day
No matter what I do or see
No, I'll not forget the day
When Jesus spoke to me

I no longer have a donkey
My childhood days have passed away
But I still hear His words
And shall 'til my dying day
Did I go to the stable
Or was it a young child's dreams?
It matters not, for I heard His word
And I live by what He means.

Dennis Packham

CHILDREN'S CHRISTMAS VERSE

Let us every person
Sing, dance, pray and play
With whatever you want to pray for
For Christ is born
O la la O la la

Remember forever
Christ fed, cured
And gave dignity
To every human being

Sing, dance, pray and play
O la la O la la
For Christ is born

As you grow
You can get guidance
From him while alive
And as well as deed
Christ is forever
To those who want him

Ghazanfer Eqbal

HOPE

Oh! I hope Daddy's home for Christmas
Mummy said, he might pay the rent
Oh! I hope Daddy's home for Christmas
And the money's not all spent.

Oh! I hope Daddy's home for Christmas
And he stays off the drink
Mum said she's got him socks
But his feet will still stink.

Oh! I hope Daddy's home for Christmas
And he brings me a better present
than last year.
He gave me a dolly in bits
And I ended up in tears.

Oh! I hope Daddy's home for Christmas
I don't want anything else
Just to see Mum and him cuddle
Is a present in itself.

Phillip A Taylor

THE SCHOOL CHRISTMAS PARTY

Sisters Jody and Sophie are going to the school Christmas party,
After deciding what to wear, Mum helped them to get ready.
Ten year old Jody chose trousers and a pretty sparkly top,
Sophie is six and decided to wear her purple velvet party frock.

In the bedroom the girls dressed and towelled wet hair,
With talcum powder and clothes scattered everywhere.
They chatted excitedly about having refreshments and a disco too,
Jody and Sophie love to dance, especially with their friends at school.

The girls were nearly ready, when suddenly they started arguing,
'What's the matter?' asked Mum noticing Sophie was nearly crying.
'Jody has more money for refreshments than me,' cried Sophie,
'It's alright' Mum replied, 'You shall have the same as Jody.'

Peace was soon restored, the sisters were smiling again,
'Now hurry.' said Mum, 'It's time to go, your friends will be waiting.'
The girls looked quite beautiful, at last they were ready,
Dad was taking them in the car, he said, 'Enjoy the party.'

The school hall looked brilliant with balloons and decorations,
A huge Christmas tree sparkled, and disco lights were flashing.
Jody and Sophie had a wonderful time at the party,
And wearing party hats went home tired but very happy.

Lorna June Burdon

HOW MUCH I LOVE CHRISTMAS

The angels singing, the Christmas bells ringing
Decorated trees, how lovely can it be
Carols being sung how beautifully done
Milk and mince pies put out for Santa
And a carrot for the reindeer too
Santa dashing in his sleigh
It's Christmas, way-hey.

Rebecca Haslam (9)

POOR DADDY CHRISTMAS

Poor Daddy Christmas
is very round
his sack is very big
he rides his sleigh
to my house
but he can't get in
we have no chimney
and only little windows
so he can't climb in
maybe he can make himself very slim
and come through the letterbox
or slide under the door
or maybe magic dust
that makes him just appear
poor Daddy Christmas
I hope he can find his way in

Gabby Copperstone

A Pun For Christmas

Here's a little Christmas ditty:
Once in Royal David's City,
Good King Wenceslas looked down
When he heard a certain sound -
A pitter-patter. With delight,
He cried out in the Silent Night:
'D'you hear those footsteps? Rudolph's here.'
'No,' said his wife, 'that's just rain, dear!'

Roger Williams

CHRISTMAS

Santa Claus is busy making toys
For all the little girls and boys.
Cars, boats and lots of games,
To play indoors if it should rain
Dolls, teddy bears and puppy dogs,
Monkeys, rabbits and jumping frogs.
They have to be packed and named,
Making sure no two are the same.

Coloured lights have to be put on the trees,
To make them look pretty for all to see.
Chocolate, sweets and nuts too,
And lots of toffees for us to chew.
But there is a lot of work to be done,
Before we can start to have fun.
We must write all our Christmas cards out,
And check the addresses if we are in doubt.

As Christmas gets near we wonder if it will snow,
Or just rain and have the cold winds that blow.
But making a snowman would be such fun,
Seeing how quick we could get it done.
But playing snowballs we must be aware,
We could break a window if we don't take care.
On Christmas Eve stockings and pillow cases,
Will be watched for a while by eager faces.

But while you are happy and having fun
Remember it won't be the same for everyone
For some people will feel sad,
As not everyone has a mam and dad
So if you are lucky and have yours,
Don't forget to help them with the chores,
And when you go to bed Christmas night,
Let's hope your day has turned out alright.

Eileen Kyte

Santa's Poem

Santa slid down chimney small
'A Merry Christmas to you all.'
Merrily smiling, eyes twinkling
Another bag of gifts he brings.
Now he fills the stockings full
Toys, puppets with strings to pull
'Ho ho' laughs Santa, smiling bright,
'A Merry Christmas and to all goodnight.'

Joanna Till (12)

DICKIE'S BRICK

Last Christmas, as I recall, Dickie was rather sick.
He didn't get the bike he had asked for, but he did get a brick.
It wasn't made by Duplo or Lego or anything like that,
But it was just like the brick that he had tied to Auntie Jean's pet cat.
He was so cheesed off, he shouted *'What a dirty rotten trick.*
Giving a boy for Christmas an engineering brick!'
And then began to remember all about the nasty things he did,
And all those impractical jokes he always played on his
Great Uncle Sid.

He has put a brick in his carrier and his uncle dragged it for miles.
He had put a brick in his sandwich box, yes, that really made
Dickie smile.
Early on Sunday mornings, when his uncle was still in bed,
He would cycle past his prefab and lob one at his old tin shed.
Then on Great Uncle Sid's birthday, he produced the perfect fake,
He iced and decorated a house brick and said it was a birthday cake.
And I guess that Santa's fairies had a word with him about young Dick,
'Forget the multispeed mountain bike, deliver young Dick a brick.'

Now you should pay heed to this story, only do the things you should.
You know it's not long until Christmas, so be kind, don't fib
And be good.

Gary J Cox

CHRISTMAS BAZAAR

Nina knitted a snowman,
She got in a mess with his head:
She tried to unravel her knitting,
And pulled out her jumper instead.

Simon was sewing a Santa,
He sewed till his fingers, they hurt.
He used such a long piece of cotton,
He stitched Santa onto his shirt.

Paula had problems with glitter,
She spilt it all over the place.
Peter had problems with glue-sticks,
There was glitter all over his face.

Martin was mixing the pastry
To make the mince pies for the teas.
The flour bag burst when he dropped it,
And everyone started to sneeze.

Megan spent hours on an angel,
Putting lacy bits onto each wing.
Her work is so slow and so careful,
She might get it finished - by spring.

Penny was painting a reindeer:
She went rather mad with the paint.
When she'd covered the floor and ceiling,
Our teacher collapsed in a faint.

> We all got covered in glitter and glue,
> And flour, paint and paper as well.
> It took us a week to clear it all up -
> *But we made lots of things to sell!*

Jennifer Bailey

ONE NIGHT I LAY WONDERING . . .

What if Father Christmas was just too late
For all the calls he has to make?
What if his reindeer went on strike?
Snorting 'You're not getting us to budge tonight.'

Or Father Christmas got stuck in our chimney?
Or on a night dark and windy,
His sleigh slipped down our frosty roof,
His sack burst open, the toys fell loose?

And train sets and dolls' prams fell past my window,
Jigsaws and teddy bears and hundreds of Lego,
And Santa and reindeer landed all of a heap,
But Mum'd say 'That's silly! Now get off to sleep.'

Margaret Gregory

THE BEARDED FATMAN

Ho! Ho! Ho! Hear my jolly cheer,
Ho! Ho! Ho! It's that time of year
For me, the bearded fatman in his coat of red
To bath all the reindeer and polish up the sled.

All my little workers are ready for a rest,
Now it's up to me to complete my yearly quest
Of travelling round the world delivering all the toys
They'd worked so hard to make for all the girls and boys

This year Ho! Ho! I nearly came unstuck
And had to part with money to hire an Eddie Stobart truck.
Mrs Christmas, bless her, deary, deary me,
Forgot to get the sled its annual MOT.

What's more, Rudolph poor chap, went and caught a cold,
And feeling proper poorly wouldn't do as he was told.
I poured some horrid medicine right down his sore throat,
He then spat it back at me, all down my best red coat.

Never fear dear children, everything's turned out right
And I will get away on time and that very special night.
So, don't forget to leave me some milk and bread and cheese
If you want to find your presents underneath your Christmas trees.

Keith Farley

THE MAGIC OF CHRISTMAS

As Christmas Day draws ever near and carollers sing loud and clear,
the festive season is begun with cards despatched and shopping done.
First, carefully prepared and baked, a richly fruited Christmas cake
is iced . . . within its sugar-snow, tree, sleigh and Santa in a row.

Whilst decorations wait beneath the tinselled tree, a Yuletide wreath
is hung to ornament the door, providing welcoming décor
for visitors who come and go, scanning skies for signs of snow,
delivering parcels, neatly penned, addressed to relative or friend.

Young children study, eyes agog, fruit tartlets, mince pies, chocolate
                                                                                               log,
balloons, lights, fir tree, coloured balls, crackers,
                            garland-festooned walls,
mistletoe, holly, angel, bells and aromatic candle smells.
Smiles beam each time a glance locates nuts, chocolates, sweets,
                                                fresh fruit and dates.

Excitement mounts on Christmas Eve for eager children who believe
that reindeer, guiding Santa's sleigh, fly, bringing gifts for
                                                Christmas Day.
They go to bed, refuse to sleep, resolve to stay awake and peep
for they're determined to catch sight of Santa when he calls that night.

But, finally, the Sandman wins and, silently, hard work begins
with parcels beside beds to stack, or pile in special Christmas sack.
No creaks, no squeaks - a stealthy tread - no noise must wake
                                                the child in bed
to break the spell and drive away the magic of this unique day.

At dawn's first light, to laughs and squeals, each unwrapped package
                                                                        now reveals
its hidden gift to sparkling eyes when every curious child unties
a knotted string or coloured bow to greet all finds with gasps of 'Oh!'
And so, with Christmas Day begun, the time has come for festive fun
as church bells peal across the earth, reminding of the
                                                  Saviour's birth.

Maureen Atkin

CHRISTMAS LIGHTS

Christmas Eve comes and magic is flowing,
Along the High Street lanterns are glowing,
All around the Christmas tree sparkling - glitter,
Christmas lights, fairy lights, candles flicker,
Gleam and glisten in the cold frosty air,
But no tinsel glory is ever as bright,
As the star studded sky on this special night.

Ivy Allpress

HICKORY DICKORY SOCKS

Hickory dickory dock
Santa has lost his socks
He is running around
With his trousers half down.
Though his toes do not show
The winter wind doth blow.

Hickory dickory dock
Santa's wearing a frock
He is stuck high tonight
In the dazzling moonlight.
Rudolph has gone to knock
He's now picking the lock,
Inside he's found Santa's
Pair of socks chock-a-block
Hickory dickory socks.

Marisha Rose

CHRISTMAS IS NEAR

Little James is praying,
For a garage full with cars.
Mummy is saying,
'You'll have to write to Santa Claus.'
Jane wants a baby doll,
To dress with lots of different clothes,
Jane is only four years old,
Her brother she loathes.
He is eight years old.
A baby doll is something that Jane yearns for,
She wishes for it with all her heart and soul.
While James longs for lots of cars,
He also wants a lorry with big wheels.
Christmas is getting near
At last it is Christmas Eve
There is lots of good cheer,
Santa Claus will soon leave,
To deliver presents far and near.
Yes Christmas is nearly here.

Jacqueline Darts

CHRISTMAS TIME

At Christmas time
You eat lots of pudding
That is very creamy
Just to eat
Delicious meat
Turkey and stuffing
Singing at the table
Laughing and drinking
Having lots of fun

Stars are sparkling in the sky
They are very very high
They are shining out so very bright
Tiny and large in the night
It really is a lovely sight.

Julie Birkenfield (15)

A Christmas Poem

Christmas time is here
The trees are prickly
My nose feels tickly

When the pudding is cooking

It is very hot
And is sitting
In a great big pot.

Big presents, small presents
Fat presents too
I like playing with all of them
Because they are new.

Kelly Duncan (15)

CHRISTMAS

The robin is bobbin'
And the trees are white
Christmas is coming
Around tonight.

The presents get wrapped
The food gets cooked
It will all be demolished
After just one look.

The star is sparkly
In the sky
Shining down
From away up high.

Louise Lothian (14)

Santa

Santa Claus is big and fat
He gives presents to kids at night
He has a bushy beard
And rides on a sledge
In the sky at night.

Every day he slides down a chimney
And leaves a present under the tree
Only if the kids are asleep
So never never get up at night
Or Santa will go
And not leave you a present at all.

Sean Smith (14)

CHRISTMAS LIST

At Christmas time
You get loads of presents
And in them
You may get
Two Gameboys
Two cats
Two watches
Two balls
Two bats
Two rats
Two books
Two dolls
And of course
A TV set
When you open them you feel very good
You feel very cheerful
Because you've been good
If you've been bad
You might get coal
Not what you want
So watch out.

Julie Cranston (15)

CHRISTMAS

At Christmas
We have presents
Sitting under the tree
Some are for you
And some are for me.

We eat lots of food
And we get so fat
With turkey, sausages and crisps
That we squash the cat.

The tree is prickly
With branches tall and thin
Covered with decorations
And sitting in a bin.

Natalie Lennox (14)

WHAT IF?

What if we left the fire still glowing the evening Santa was
due to come,
and when he came sliding down the chimney the embers
burned his bum.

What if the girls missed the Christmas party and the presents
they could choose,
'cos we sneaked in very quietly and locked them in the loos.

What if the teacher was walking down the playground and didn't
duck in time,
and the snowball thrown by my best friend covered him in slime.

What if the snowman's carrot nose only put in on Christmas Eve,
was eaten by a reindeer just as Santa was away to leave.

What if when we were singing carols, sniggering and trying to
keep in time,
I forgot what verse we were on and sung completely the wrong line.

What if Santa got slightly mixed up the night he came to call,
instead of leaving a train set, he left a girlie's doll.

What if we forgot about Christmas, or Santa once came late,
I hope that never happens, 'cos I think Christmas time is great.

Christopher Leith

GOOD CHEER

Snowbells in the air, fog in the close.
Who are we waiting for? Santa Claus.
Full is our stocking up to the hilt,
Nice lovely weather for wearing a kilt.

Why don't you lay off vodka and whisky?
Nothing like milk for making you frisky!
Bring in the hot pies, cakes and scones,
Let us be merry as Christmas Day dawns.

Is your chimney swept, kept nice and clean?
Are children all snug midst blankets between?
All the gifts and presents are here.
Christ in the manger, nothing to fear!

So the story is told of a child,
Told to the shepherds out in the wild.
All of the angels sing in the choir.
Hark! All the singing comes from afar.

Mary the name of the virgin is given.
Gabriel the angel sent down from heaven.
God on his throne up there in the sky.
A babe is born for both you and I.

So at this time of feast and song,
Let nothing ever be done wrong.
To all the world the Gospel tell,
As we ring out the Christmas bell.

Thomas W Splitt

IT'S CHRISTMAS AGAIN

I fly with my reindeer,
I sit on my sleigh,
I land on roofs,
I slide down the chimneys,
I give them presents,
They give me food and drink sometimes,
That's *my* Christmas.

Shaune Carey

CHRISTMAS

C is for the Christmas choir;
H is for the bright green holly;
R is for red robins;
I is for invitations;
S is for the snowy weather;
T is for the glowing trees;
M is for Merry Christmas;
A is for Advent calendars;
S is for Santa Claus giving out the presents.

Vicky Harbour (10)

CHRISTMAS

Christmas is here
The snow falls to the ground
Families gather to celebrate
The tinsel shines on the tree
The fairy looks down upon us
Everyone is having a good time.

Lewanne Mudd (10)

CHRISTMAS

Christmas is a time when Jesus was born
Christmas is a time when all the family meet
We all have Christmas dinner
A really special treat.

Jonathan Wilcox (10)

A Christmas Poem

Right in his sleigh,
The Father lay,
Ready for his travelling he goes,
With his cold he's got a big red nose.
Rudolph is his name,
As he travels he shouts.
'Now Dasher! Now Dancer! Now Prancer and Vixen!
On, Comet! On, Cupid! On, Donner and Blitzen!'
As he arrives he falls down the chimney covered in soot,
When he speaks with his mouth full it comes out like 'Apoot!'
When he flies,
He vanishes in the skies,
So his name is
Santa!

Robert Prior

CHRISTMAS IN BLOOM

Blooming Christmas Day's been nigh
(So it seems) since 1st July.
Blooming crowded shopping malls,
Jingle Bells and Barbie dolls,
Blooming Spice Girls' latest hit
(Blooming word that rhymes with 'twit'),
Blooming kiss from Great Aunt Flo,
Blooming (blooming!) mistletoe,
Blooming socks from Auntie Jane
(Blooming pink and black . . . again),
Blooming Christmas songs to sing
(What's this blooming 'wassailing'?)
Blooming turkey, heaving muscles,
Blooming (blooming!) sprouts from Brussels,
Blooming Pantos bore me, too
(Oh no, they don't? *Oh yes, they do!*)
Blooming Santa Claus - who's he?
(Blooming hope he visits me).

David E W Walker

HAPPY CHRISTMAS

Happy Christmas to you
Angels made your dreams come true
Peace and solace for everyone
Presents too giving you lots of fun
Yuletide carollers come to your door
Crystal tones rejoice for evermore
Harps and violins harmoniously play
Rings of laughter make your day
Inside the fire warms the fingers and toes
Silently outside the snow and wind blows
Turkey and stuffing flow into your tummy
Mince pies and cake yet to come - yummy
A light that brightly shines is a sign
Santa and Rudolph have come to dine.

Catriona McNicoll

I Don't Like Sprouts

Lovely roast turkey stuffing too,
But I don't like sprouts!
Roast potatoes all crisp and golden,
But I don't like sprouts!
Sausages wrapped in bacon,
But I don't like sprouts!
Mum just said 'There's no sprouts!'
There are broad beans instead
But . . .!

Jessica Sutton

IT'S CHRISTMAS TIME

It's Christmas time,
A time for giving,
A joyful , pleasing time of year,
It fills me with excitement
When I think of snow, holly and mistletoe,
Children get excited waiting for Santa Claus to visit.
It would be a shame to miss it,
Stars sparkle and glitter,
Christmas is near,
Hooray, I like this time of year!

Kirsty Williams

CHRISTMAS IS NEAR!

Christmas is near!
Come over here!
Look what I've got!
A lovely pot,
Guess what's in it?
Well, it's a fixing kit,
What do you want a fixing kit for?
Oh! It's for next door!
Who lives there?
A bear!
A bear?
What does he want it for?
His door,
His door?
Yes of course!

Jazzy H

THE CHRISTMAS BRAINSTORM

At Christmas Santa Claus carries a sack.
He carries it on his back.
He has lots of things in his sack
But he still carries it on his back.
The elves make the things in the sack
But Santa Claus still carries it on his back.
He goes down the chimney with the sack.
Then *finally takes it off his back!*

Sarah Fox

It's Christmas Time

It's Christmas morning, boy oh boy!
I hope I get a smashing toy,
Santa riding in his sleigh,
Did he visit me today?

Lots of presents by the tree,
Is that big one there for me?
Santa came to us for sure,
Is he still outside the door?

Look at my presents,
Aren't they neat,
All there for my *special* treat
These Christmas presents you just can't beat.

Ashley Jeggo

A Christmas Poem

Santa has a sack,
Which he carries in the back
Of his great big sledge,
Which flies over the hedge.
Hurry up Blitzen,
And help poor Vixen.

Down the chimney he goes,
And lands on his toes,
Puts the presents around,
Then he leaves with a bound,
Hurry up Prancer,
And help poor Dancer.

Sarah Bolton

CHRISTMAS POEM

Christmas is great!
Especially when Santa comes
With his sack of toys.
It's a special time of year
For all the girls and boys.
Then Santa puts some toys
In every girl and boy's stocking.

Then morning time came
And the children rushed down
They opened their presents one by one,
And they said 'Thank you Santa
Wherever you are.'

Rachel Halcrow

CHRISTMAS POEM

Coming down from the chimney
Ever so quick came St Nick,
With a sack on his back,
Full of toys,
For little boys and girls,
As quick as a flash!
Rudolph went dash,
And off he flew,
In the night of blue,
With Prancer and
Dancer
And Vixen and Dasher,
And Donner and Blitzen.

Sian Major

ON CHRISTMAS EVE LONG AGO

On Christmas Eve long ago,
I thought I heard a *'Ho! Ho! Ho!*
The curtains swayed and I was afraid,
I was too scared to say 'Hello.'
I never did see who it was that night,
But I did see a bright light.
A glow of red, I buried my head
'Who was it?' I said to myself in my bed.
I bet it was Santa Claus somehow or other,
Because there were presents for me and my brother.

DouglasBeattie

CHRISTMASTIME

At Christmastime
Carol singers in the snow,
How their lanterns love to glow.

Reindeer flying through the sky,
Santa's hoping for a mince pie.

Presents under the Christmas tree,
I wonder if there will be one for me?

Christmas comes but once a year,
When we remember all those who are dear.

Matthew Willis

THE BAND COMES

the trumpets blare and
saxophones in trees
their shrill sounds
roar from loudspeakers

the small mice fly
from noises high
to farms nearby

they scamper under doors
around the skirting boards
then under beds and chairs
they hide

a loud bang on the
drum the band has
come

Richard Stoker

HAPPY CHRISTMAS MOTHER

I dream about you often, Mother.
Just maybe we could both discover,
That we could get along somehow,
If only you were still here now.

I think of you each Boxing Day,
When we celebrate your birthday.
Too young your life came to an end,
Before I was able to be your friend.

I loved you more than I told you so,
But you didn't seem to want to know.
I believe you are in Heaven above,
Safe in the arms of my God of love.

One day there I might understand,
When we meet in the Heavenly Land,
Why you made me suffer so badly;
Then I will listen to you gladly.

No-one on Earth could replace you,
Alone in the hard times to ensue,
When I desperately needed a mother,
To help me to cope and then recover.

You have four great-grandchildren
And I know you would adore them.
In turn they ask me all about you.
They enjoy seeing your photos too.

Mother, as another Christmas nears,
I think about all our missing years.
Please wait for me in Heaven above;
I dedicate this to you with my love.

Janet Hewitt

FROM CHARLETTE'S ARK TO JESUS CHRIST

Me and Bubbles are all but two now
It's been two short years since we met you,
But you are nineteen hundred and ninety eight
That's an awful lot of years to do.

Gabrielle and Goldilocks
Hold a feather up to you,
Jessica still holds her rose
While Sad Sam cries to you.

Here inside our little home
Have houses, paintings, gifts from you,
And all the animals are happy
When all the tears are over too.

But when it comes to Christmas Day
Out come all the dolls to play
All the teddies sit to tea
Dumpy, Poppet, Bubbles and me.

And we shall light the Christmas candles
And play some Christmas carols too
And this year's crib is in a boat
Well didn't you come for fishermen too?

And we know Jesus Christ is busy
Especially on Christmas Day,
But we'd like to invite you round to dinner
As 'Honoured Guest' on Christmas Day.

Charlette de Christi

CHILDREN'S CHRISTMAS VERSE

As Santa got stuck in the chimney,
he began to wriggle and shout,
pushing here and pushing there,
he was so worried he couldn't get out,
but as he pushed down came the soot
and there was Santa looking more like the
                                      chimney sweeper!

G A Pocock

CHRISTMAS IS HERE

The holly is prickly
The berry is red.

The dinner is tasty
The pudding fruity.

Christmas is cheerful
The children are excited.

The star is bright
It is very shiny.

The tree branches are busy
The decorations are glittery

Robin Redbreast sitting on a tree
Singing a song for Christmas.

Santa is fat and jolly
Delivering presents.

His reindeer's nose
Is like a red bulb.

Lots of things happen
Christmas is here.

Laura Jane Cumming (14)

SANTA

Santa is a fat man
With a red nose
He gives people presents
In his red clothes
He has a bushy beard
And a reindeer too
He rides on a sledge
And visits me and you.

Colin Kwok (14)

IT IS CHRISTMAS

Christmas is exciting for kids,
We like Christmas because we get presents,
We get good food and turkey,
We see friends and the family,
We hang up decorations,
And have a Christmas tree,
We have lots of fun
at Christmastime.

Deen Lawrence

CHRISTMAS

Sending presents,
Receiving presents,
Joy all around,
Decorations all around,
Joy, joy to all families,
Excitement there,
Excitement here,
Excitement everywhere.

Kevin Filmer

Santa's Grotto

All I want for Christmas
Is to meet Santa Claus
To see him in his grotto
In one of the big stores

Santa will ask me my name
And sit me upon his knee
He will ask have I been good
Then he will give a present to me

I asked Santa for a porcelain doll
With beautiful golden hair
Then I asked for another gift
Which was a teddy bear.

There's so much to see in the grotto
It looks like a fairyland
But Mummy says 'It's time to go'
And gently takes my hand.

I put my presents gently under the Christmas tree
Wondering is it a porcelain doll
Or maybe a teddy bear
That Santa gave to me.

Annette Carver

SINGING YO-HO-HO FROM SANTA!

Santa Claus spends all year
Filling every sack,
He doesn't mind hard work
Has the knack to pack and stack
A toy for each and everyone
Who's good and likes some fun,
Singing Yo-Ho-Ho! from Santa and Yo-Ho-Ho! from me!
Singing Yo-Ho-Ho! from Reindeer, another Yo-Ho-Ho! from me!

Santa Claus supplies gifts
Speeding thro' the night,
Rallying lively reindeer
Dusk to dawn delivery flight,
Hurtling to each and everyone
Who's good and likes some fun,
Singing Yo-Ho-Ho! from Santa and Yo-Ho-Ho! from me!
Singing Yo-Ho-Ho! from Reindeer, another Yo-Ho-Ho! from me!

Santa never misses
A home in any street,
Remember to leave Santa
A small drink and sweetmeat treat.
Thank you to him from everyone
Who's good and likes some fun,
Singing Yo-Ho-Ho! from Santa and Yo-Ho-Ho! from me!
Singing Yo-Ho-Ho! from Reindeer, another Yo-Ho-Ho! from me!

Homeward bound for Santa
To the North Pole is far,
His singing can be heard
As reindeer *Oompah! Oompah!*
Singing Yo-Ho-Ho! from Santa and Yo-Ho-Ho! from me!
Singing Yo-Ho-Ho! from Reindeer, another Yo-Ho-Ho! from me!

Hilary Jill Robson

CHRISTMAS EVE

All the stars come out to play
Soon it will be Christmas Day
Children's faces full of delight
What will he leave us this Christmas night?
Doll, a book, a scooter too
Mary says to Jack 'What will he leave you?'
Time for bed you sleepyheads
Morning comes early so off you go
To a land where gentle breezes blow
And when you awaken he will have been
Such a wondrous sight you've never seen.

N Carruthers

My Maker Is Greater Than My Daddy/Mommy!

I have a *Maker!*
He is not a 'heart-breaker'!
With Him each day I wake up happy
To the good things I am made of!
He is not my mommy/daddy!
He is greater than thee!
Maybe I could call *Him* my great daddy!
He is the one we cannot see
Till we His grace receive!
Yet His goodness we can feel!
He has given great spirit to me!
He is always with me saving me from rifts and harms!
First He gave the 'gift of life' to me!
He gave me two bright eyes from birth to see!
His artistic works and wonders on Earth!
Two listening ears to hear His words!
Two feet to work and walk about!
Two hands to feel and touch and help others out!
Two lips to tell of His worth!
A tongue and voice to sing His praises!
A nose to smell the perfume-scented roses in gardens and the dells!
Good health that I can always feel 'swell'!
I shall worship Him always and of His kindness tell!
I am working my way to Heaven's door
For I don't want to go to Hell
With the devil to dwell!
I don't want to be Satan's slave!
I don't want to have ungodly craze, I want to love and serve
                                   the Lord always!
Ever skipping and jumping and telling of His lovely ways!
Never from such goodness to stray!
He is the One who propels my life's progress like a ship
                                   on tossing waves!

Ciel

POPO THE CLOWN MEETS SANTA

Popo was a little clown,
That he had never met Santa
Made him frown.

So his mum and dad took him everywhere,
But each time 'That's not the real Santa,'
In tears he'd declare.

Everyone searched here and there, high and low,
For the real Santa,
But still Popo's tears did flow.

Then that night while Popo slept,
Upon tiptoes,
Into his room someone crept.

Giving Popo a gentle shake,
The little clown,
Was soon awake.

'Santa!' little Popo cried
And taking the little clown's hand,
Through the window both did glide.

Together they delivered presents all through the night,
Until the last one was gone
And it was nearly daylight.'

Patting Popo on the head,
Santa thanked him for his help
And delivered him safely back to his bed.

Later when Popo told his mum and dad,
They laughed and said,
It was a dream he'd had.

But when the real Santa came to tea,
On that Christmas Day,
Amazed they looked at Popo and everyone
                laughed and danced with glee.

Sheila Valerie Baldwin

CHRISTMASTIME

Christmastime brings true magic, when little ones are around,
It's lovely to see their faces and to hear their happy sound.
Until one has a small one who you should always remember,
You may say quietly to yourself, I wish there was no December.

I'm afraid I was never blessed like some,
And was able to make a little home.
But I often worked amongst the young,
And wherever I went there were always some.

Having now been retired for many years,
I've seen more of little ones than some of my peers.
Whilst working I was on duty either Christmas or Boxing Day,
So in that area I had to stay.

Now when invited I go away,
And kiddies often brighten the day.
Children have never bothered me,
The younger ones always fill me with glee.

Last year where I did go,
There were many who would have liked to steal the show,
But the little one who did that, I fear,
Was one of my great nephews, under a year.

Luckily the other children were happy about this
And all were thankful for the bliss.
The others adored the little lad,
So a very happy day was had.

Betty Green

OUR CHRISTMAS EVE

Santa Claus will soon be here
Wonder if he'll bring me a teddy bear,
I would like a cuddly baby dolly
All dressed up and looking jolly.
Perhaps a book to paint and read
Or a game, and sweets, to have a good feed.
Mummy said I mustn't be greedy
We must sometimes help the needy,
And think of Baby Jesus too
It's his birthday so of course I do!
Chains and tree sparkle and shine
All our stockings hang in line
I'm so excited, I can't sleep
Will Santa really mind if I peep?
Hope he sees his milk and pie
And doesn't just pass us by,
Was that his footstep on the stairs?
I think I'll hide in case he appears.
My eyes just won't stay open now,
Must keep awake, but I don't know how!

B R Lloyd

Santa's Arrival

Santa is coming, we've waited all year
For his bright little helpers and trusty reindeer
We've dressed up the branches
And turned on the lights
We've hung out the stockings
And said our goodnights.

The carrot is ready the mince pies on hand
For travel is tiring across this vast land
Our eyes are so sleepy
Our minds cannot rest
Our beds warm and cosy
To welcome the fest.

Softly he approaches his steps sinking deep
He wonders if everyone here is asleep
'Rudolph, here's a carrot
I do like mince pies
We've got to move quickly
To leave a surprise.'

The children wake early to see what's in store
There's videos and teddies and chocolates and more
But how did he get here
In the dead of the night
When the doors are all locked
And the windows shut tight?

We don't have a chimney and Santa's too fat
To squeeze through the keyhole or under the mat
The roof fits quite snugly
There's no gap as such
There's only one answer
His magical touch!

Kay Rainsley

AUNTIE BLODWEN'S CHRISTMAS

'Where's Blod going for Christmas?'
I innocently asked my mam.
'Auntie Blodwen to you, mind,
She's staying with her cousin Sian.'

'Oh brilliant!' I can't help shouting,
I won't get dressed all day,
I'll eat chocolate in the morning
And the gang can come in to play.

Blooming different last year,
When Auntie Blod arrived,
Complete with cat and dead black hat,
Her moustaches left unshaved.

We couldn't have balloons or crackers
In case they made her jump,
And Dad had a bar on smoking his cigar
Unless he went out on the twmp.

Poor Mam couldn't have her sherry,
Because *Auntie* had signed the pledge
But I saw in her big black bag
A bottle of 'Irish Sedge'.

That cat was just as bad
Fat and bleak as her.
He dribbled on the Christmas pudding
And was never known to purr.

But hooray! She's going to Sian's house
We'll have a real good day.
The telephone rings, it changes things.
Sian has to go away.

Elizabeth Meredith

CHRISTMAS MAGIC

There's a certain night in all the year
That makes all children laugh and cheer.
The stores are filled, as it draws near,
With tinsel and toys, as little ones peer
Amazed! There are Santa's reindeer!
Joy abounds.

Christmas Eve is a birthday we celebrate,
A Baby's, who taught us to love, not to hate.
His presents were few, such was his fate,
But kings came to see Him, and no one was late
Love's around.

So remember all children on this special day
When you unwrap your parcels and fun games you play,
As love wraps around you, rejoice if you may,
That little Lord Jesus - He showed us the way.
Trumpet sounds!

M Lister

CHRISTMAS IS FOR LIFE!

'How can a baby save lost souls?
Surely he has other goals!'
'Lord Jesus saves! Just give Him time!
The end result will be sublime!
Right now, with Mary, He's got peace -
Tomorrow wisdom will increase!
One day He'll baffle everyone
And prove He really is God's Son!
Today is just a stepping stone!
Don't criticise . . . leave Him alone . . .
Just wait and see . . . you'll understand -
The day He holds you by the hand
And says He loves you right out loud!
That day you'll be so glad, so proud!
You'll praise His Name, a child of God,
Then you won't think the Lord so odd!
You'll read your Bible, say your prayers,
Rejoice with us that Jesus cares!
You'll tell your friends that you are saved!
You'll be polite, so well-behaved!
My son, you'll be a Christian, too,
And comprehend my point of view . . .
But Jesus knows of what will be -
He simply says, 'Come, trust in Me!'
It's up to you when you believe
But on that day you will receive -
Forgiveness, pardon, love and joy . . .
For now, you're just a child, a boy . . .
We'll learn together, you and I . . .
One day we'll know the answer why . . .'

Denis Martindale

THE NIGHT BEFORE CHRISTMAS

'Twas the night before Christmas
And Santa was a wreck.
He had badly sprained his ankle,
And had a sore, stiff neck.

His suit was at the cleaners
And his socks were full of holes.
His long beard needing washing,
And his boots were lacking soles.

He was behind with the wrapping
Of all the Christmas toys.
He had also mislaid the addresses
Of all the girls and boys.

Rudolf was no better -
For he was in a strop.
He'd been loading up the sleigh,
And he had let the parcels drop.

Bits and pieces were everywhere,
For some of the parcels had split.
Rudolf couldn't find the tape,
And he'd lost the mending kit.

Rudolf rushed into the house,
'Santa! I've had an idea!
Why not save us this hassle,
And cancel Christmas this year?'

Santa was in a lather,
And his face was glowing pink.
He was beginning to despair,
and about to take to drink.

'Rudolf! That's the best plan yet!'
Said Santa, now full of glee.
'You shall have some extra oats,
And I'll have a pot of tea.

I'll send an urgent message
To all the good people here,
'Sorry we couldn't make it,
But we'll try again - next year!

We'll make up a roaring fire,
Then we'll sit and have a rest.
It will mean a 'Do-It-Yourself' Christmas,
But perhaps it will be the very best - *ever!*

Julia Whale

RED AND WHITE

For me it is,
Only red and white,
At Christmas time,
That fills my sight,
White for the snow,
So soft and deep,
Red for Santa's cloak,
And from warm beds little eyes that peep,
White for the icing,
On the cake,
Red for the wine we sip,
To toast the Christmas appearance he did make,
White for the berries,
Of mistletoe,
And red for Rudolph's nose,
Scarlet scarves that around cold necks flow,
White for the shawl,
Around baby Jesus wrapped,
Red for the robin,
At your window who hungrily flapped,
White for the choirboys'
Uniformed look,
Red for their,
Christmas carol book,
White for Santa's,
Long and ancient beard,
Red for the solitary candle,
Lit at this time of the year,
Red and white,
Both dominate,
My season of goodwill,
Vividly my Christmas palette fill.

P J Littlefield

ANYTHING ELSE YOU'D LIKE TO KNOW ABOUT XMAS?

'Mummy why has Santa Claus?'
'Wrong claws dear, for example
'if' begins a different clause, conditional tense.'
'OK, 'if' Santa had claws,' she patiently persisted
'would he scratch if I tried to steal a present, not mine?'
'Now is your gift of the present, your past, your future -
present your next question darling.'
'Why are reindeer?'
'Why is rain dear, is better grammar pet . . .
. . . because deer are expensive to feed I suppose . . .
though not as expensive as petrol, or presents
- but then, you didn't ask that . . .'
'Then there's the sleigh, I thought he was kind
so why would he need to slay?'
'Ecologically better than petrol, pet.
Anything else I can help clear up for you . . .?'
. . . 'Will Santa bring a computer Mum?'
'Well love, the sleigh will be full
Rudolph is suffering from strain - all those
public appearances at supermarkets, Santa is caring
- besides computers are dear, and you are only seven.
I thought I saw him wrapping shoes your size
and maybe, if you're really good
you'll get books, paints, and a yo-yo too
Anything else you'd like to know?
Bless the babe, she's asleep
I'm glad I'm the kind of mother
who answers honesty.
Saves so much confusion when they grow up.'

I M Brown

CHRISTMAS EVE

Christmas bells in golden silence
      with fairy lights adorn the tree.
Happy children - peals of laughter -
      ring out when wrapped gifts they see.
Roused now to great excitement -
      on this eve of Christmas Day -
'I spy' they'd play at present -
      if only they could have their way!
Sandman calling - eyelids drooping -
      time tho' for a little prayer -
To thank God for His greatest gift,
      unwrapped and free - a friend to share.
Mindful ever we must be -
      of love on us God did bestow.
A Babe in cattle shed was born,
      Lord Jesus, to Him humbly bow.
Son of God who saves from sin,
      when you accept Him this you'll know.

Marian Curtis Jones

STAY COOL SANTA!

Have you ever seen a Santa with his knickers in a twist
Trying to deliver all the presents on his list?

It really isn't easy when you've got a job like that
And you know you're past it 'cause you're old and rather fat.

All the elves that help you are as naughty as can be
And the reindeer aren't too happy when they're asked to work for free.

You start to work in January but still it isn't long
To allow for all the silly things that often can go wrong.

No matter just how soon you start to make the piles of toys,
There never seems to be enough for all the girls and boys.

And then they send you letters saying 'I want this and that'
As if it's just dead easy and you whip them out of your hat!

Quick change of plan and back to work
So no-one thinks you're a mean old jerk.

No wonder that it's hectic when Christmas Eve is here
And you're loading up the sleigh with all the jolly gear!

Well, Santa. Here's a message from all of us today:
'Hang in there, stay cool, smile it out, we're with you all the way!'

C Sanderson

CHRISTMAS EVE

The snowman climbed a chimney pot
And began to get far too hot
What a muddle!
Is that a puddle?
Oh! What a terrible shock he got!

He met old Santa Klaus
Who stopped to take a pause
'You poor man!'
He began.
'Please climb aboard my horse.'

'Horse!' cried Rudolph in despair.
'You need glasses I do declare!'
'Be calm,' he said.
'There's kids in bed!
They'll wake and see us here!'

Rudolph raised his antlers.
'I'm not a horse that canters!
I'm a deer!
A flying chair!
I save you from climbing stairs.'

'I'm a silly Father Christmas!
It must be all the stress,
Lots of presents,
To be sent!
In just one night, oh what a mess!'

'Grab the reins, gee-up, we've not got long!
Hold tight, the sky's where we belong,
Tally-ho! Tally-ho!
Let's go! Let's go!
Let's sing Rudolph's song as we fly along.'

Denise Russell

UNTITLED

Jingle bells! Jingle bells!
The children let out their yells.
Rudolph's nose, oh so bright,
You can see it glowing at night.
Santa's here! Santa's here!
Let's all let out a cheer.
Over the rooftops goes his sleigh,
On and on, Santa's on his way.
Visiting children here and there.
The excitement is too much to bear.
But much too soon morning has come,
And Santa has gone to his home.

Matthew James

CHRISTMAS SURPRISE

The Christmas tree is decorated,
All bright with tinsel and bows,
A small child is laid asleep in bed,
What gifts will Santa bring, who knows?
He's dreaming of a big yellow truck,
That will carry lots of mud,
And pushing round and round the garden,
He'd be on it if he could.
Are all the best trucks yellow?
If so, I wonder why,
But still he liked the one that comes to bits,
With the crane that can touch the sky.
Next, his adventures on a pirate ship,
With a cannon and a plank,
And pirates with wooden legs and hooks,
And cabins dark and dank.
What more surprises are there in store,
In Santa's sack tonight,
As he leaves the parcels on the floor,
And disappears in the twinkle of a light?

Pam Cook

CHRISTMAS TREE SONG

Dance, dance, dance with me
Under the bright green Christmas tree.
Chant, chant, chant this rhyme,
Sing it aloud at Christmas time.

While the children are in their beds
Pixies dance around their heads,
Catching dreams to take, they say
To Santa's grotto far away.

There the dreams become real things
Like toys and sweets and golden rings,
And one may become a pure White Dove
That brings its messages of love.

So dance, dance, dance with me
Under the bright green Christmas tree,
For when you wake on Christmas Day
The pixies will take your cares away.

Linda Anne Landers

IF IT WERE ME

To win the lottery would be my dream,
As countless others could be keen.
What would I do? The question hangs.
It needs some thought, this Aladdin's cave.

Some lofty thoughts at first emerge,
To save the world and all concerned.
Then down to Earth my thoughts converge,
To find a cause with merit and worth.

Family and friends, I would favour too.
There would still be enough for me and you.
Methinks for all I would care to achieve,
Winning the lottery would be the 'bee's knees'

Patricia Cure

THE MAGI

Magical mysterious was
the coming of that star
in its rising and its shining
as it guided from afar.

By day through scorching desert
and freezing cold by night
it went before us streaming
its radiant sparkling light -

Through mountains and through canyons
it lead our camelcade
until we reached the dwelling
in which the child was laid -

Our gifts of gold and incense
and perfumes from the east
we offered Him in homage
for Christ the King to feast.

And there to sound of angels
we saw his reign begin
and though we gave him rarest gifts
we left more rich within.

Rosemary Keith

THOUGHTS ABOUT CHRISTMAS

Winter morning
Freezing and cold
It is like a football ground
Chilly and old.

Stockings hanging
From the bed
I am so excited
I hit my head.

A chicken came to talk to me
I invited him for dinner
He didn't realise
He would end up in a pot
And not be a winner.

Christmas is better going then coming
Don't need to spend any money
You can sit inside all by yourself
And enjoy some bread and honey.

Steven Donoghue

SUBMISSIONS INVITED
SOMETHING FOR EVERYONE

POETRY NOW '99 - Any subject, any style, any time.

WOMENSWORDS '99 - Strictly women, have your say the female way!

STRONGWORDS '99 - Warning! Age restriction, must be between 16-24, opinionated and have strong views. (Not for the faint-hearted)

All poems no longer than 30 lines.
Always welcome! No fee!
Cash Prizes to be won!

Mark your envelope (eg *Poetry Now) '99*
Send to:
Forward Press Ltd
1-2 Wainman Road, Woodston,
Peterborough, PE2 7BU

**OVER £10,000 POETRY PRIZES
TO BE WON!**

Judging will take place in October 1999